The Legacy Blueprint:

A Guide to Bringing Generational Wealth Within Reach

MONIQUE D. HAYES

ISBN: 979-8-9886577-0-5

For permissions requests or inquiries, please contact:
Monique D. Hayes
153 E. Flagler St., #405
Miami, FL 33131
Info@moniquedhayes.com

To connect: www.moniquedhayes.com

For more information, please visit www.estatesmadeeasy.com Or follow @estatesmadeeasy on all social media platforms.

To my sister, Sonja, who has preserved and protected my family's legacy.

CONTENTS

Preface

My family suffered the devastating loss of both my mother and one of my brothers in unexpected tragedies, within one year. My brother, 2 years my elder, was the victim of gun violence that plagues much of America. My mother, who suffered from heart disease, never recovered from the loss of my brother. She died of a broken heart within months of his passing. Neither my mother nor my brother had a will at the time of their passing.

In our grief, we found ourselves overwhelmed by the legal, administrative, and tax issues that follow the death of a loved one. We struggled to get a handle on my mother's financial accounts and what to do with her home. We also struggled to understand what rights, if any, we had to access and participate in the lives of our brother's two young children. In addition, at the time my brother passed away, he was party to an ongoing lawsuit. Gaining insight and control over their affairs was a tremendous task.

This was happening although I was a practicing lawyer and had worked in the court system for years. Up until that point, my practice had centered on business law-specifically corporate restructuring. Still, because I was the lawyer in the family-everyone looked to me to understand and manage the legal issues we faced following the death of our loved ones. I knew absolutely nothing about estate planning, probate, or family law.

After that experience, I set out to learn all I could about estate planning and probate law. I wanted to ensure my family would never again find itself ill-prepared for loss. I studied the law, but I also studied people and how they process grief and make family and financial decisions while enduring grief. I examined the psychological and emotional hurdles that often-become barriers to planning. And, I explored the impact cultural, racial, and socioeconomic dynamics have on estate planning accessibility. Finally, I studied wealth and how it has historically been passed across generations-often as a resource, but sometimes as a burden.

I learned that my family's experience was not unique. More than 60% of Americans, irrespective of their access to wealth, don't have a will or other form of estate planning document. As a result, much is lost to unnecessary disputes, fees, and expenses. For the middle class and communities of color, the statistical deficit and negative impact are much greater.

- 70% of African Americans don't have a will or estate plan;

- The number of Latinx reporting they want, but don't know how to obtain a will has tripled;

- Less than 50% of the people making $80,000+ have estate planning documents despite recognizing the importance of planning.

*Source: Caring.com 2020 Estate Planning and Wills Study.

ABUNDANCE IS YOUR BIRTHRIGHT

Chapter One: Understanding Estate Planning

Estate planning is not just about transferring wealth; it's about leaving a legacy of love, guidance, and protection for those you cherish.

Introduction

Estate planning is a crucial component of any lasting financial legacy. Indeed, for those on a journey for wealth and interested in ensuring that their wealth is preserved and protected across generations, estate planning is the foundation upon which the legacy rests. But it is important to appreciate that the legacy is about more than just dollars and cents. It encompasses the values, work ethic, wisdom, and principles that have sustained the family and facilitated success over the years. Estate planning is certainly important for middle-class and high-net-worth individuals who want to leave a financial legacy for their children. But irrespective of whether you are a parent, estate planning is essential to ensure that your assets are distributed according to your wishes, your loved ones are taken care of, and your priorities are honored. In this chapter, we'll cover the basics of estate planning and provide an overview of the key legal documents involved.

But first, it is important to note, estate planning is not just for the wealthy and aging. Estate planning is for anyone who wants to protect their loved ones, pass on their assets and values, and leave a positive impact on future generations.

In many ways, estate planning can be a complex and emotional process. The complexities are often compounded by factors such as:

1. **Family Dynamics:** Estate planning involves making decisions about the distribution of assets and appointing individuals to important roles, such as executors, trustees, or guardians. These decisions can sometimes lead to conflicts and tensions within families, especially when there are differing opinions or expectations among family members.

2. **Financial Considerations:** Estate planning requires a thorough assessment of one's assets, debts, and financial goals. Determining how to distribute wealth, minimize taxes, and provide for future generations can be intricate and may involve complex legal and financial strategies.

3. **Legal Complexity:** Estate planning involves navigating various legal frameworks, including estate laws, tax laws, probate laws, and trust laws. Each jurisdiction may have its own specific rules and regulations, adding to the complexity of the process. Understanding these laws and ensuring compliance can be challenging for individuals without legal expertise.

4. **Emotional Attachments:** Individuals may have strong emotional attachments to their assets and properties, making it difficult to make decisions about their eventual transfer or distribution. Deciding who will inherit certain items or properties can be emotionally charged, as people may want to preserve family heirlooms or ensure that their loved ones are provided for.

5. **End-of-Life Considerations:** Estate planning also involves addressing end-of-life decisions, such as healthcare preferences, life support, and funeral arrangements. These discussions can be emotionally challenging as individuals confront their own mortality and grapple with difficult choices.

6. **Evolving Circumstances:** Estate planning is not a one-time event but a process that needs to be revisited and updated as circumstances change. Life events such as marriages, divorces, births, deaths, business ventures, or changes in financial status may require adjustments to the estate plan. This ongoing evaluation can add complexity and emotional strain.

7. **Legacy and Intergenerational Wealth:** Many individuals want to leave a legacy and ensure that their wealth is used in a way that aligns with their values and goals. Determining how to create a lasting impact and pass on family values through financial assets can be a deeply personal and emotional aspect of estate planning.

Given these considerations, it is understandable that estate planning can be a difficult and emotional process. Seeking the advice of estate planning professionals such as attorneys and financial advisors can assist individuals in navigating these complexities and dealing with the emotional aspects involved. These experts can offer valuable expertise, objective advice, and assistance in developing an estate plan that addresses both the practical and emotional needs of individuals and their families.

Illustration

Imagine a family consisting of parents, Sean and Jazmine, and their two children, Kyle and Victoria. Sean and Jazmine have worked hard throughout their lives, accumulating assets and building a comfortable life for their family. Unfortunately, tragedy strikes unexpectedly, and both Sean and Jazmine pass away in a car accident.

Without an estate plan in place, the family is thrown into turmoil. Kyle and Victoria, still grieving the loss of their parents, now face uncertainty and confusion regarding the distribution of their parents' assets. There is no clear guidance on who should manage the assets, pay outstanding debts, or provide for the children's ongoing care and education.

Since Sean and Jazmine did not specify their wishes, the family becomes susceptible to potential conflicts among relatives, as everyone has their own opinions on how the assets should be divided. The lack of clarity and legal direction leads to emotional strain and potential strain on family relationships.

Had Sean and Jazmine taken the time to create an estate plan, the situation could have been significantly different. With a properly executed plan, they could have appointed a trusted individual, such as a family member or close friend, as the guardian for Kyle and Victoria. This would provide peace of mind knowing that their children would be cared for by someone they chose and trusted.

Additionally, the estate plan would have outlined the distribution of assets, ensuring that Kyle and Victoria are financially secure and provided for. It could have designated a trusted executor to manage the assets and handle any outstanding debts, preventing unnecessary delays and potential mismanagement.

Moreover, an estate plan could have addressed any potential tax implications, helping to minimize estate taxes and preserve more of the family's wealth for Kyle and Victoria's future. By strategically utilizing trusts, gifting strategies, and other estate planning tools, Sean and Jazmine could have taken advantage of tax-saving opportunities and ensured a smooth transfer of wealth to their children.

Overall, this illustration emphasizes the importance of having an estate plan. It not only provides clear instructions and legal guidance for the distribution of assets but also helps protect loved ones during difficult times. By taking proactive steps to create an estate plan, parents can ensure that their wishes are followed, their loved ones are cared for, and their hard-earned assets are preserved for future generations.

What is Estate Planning?

The process of arranging for the management and distribution of your assets after your death is known as estate planning. It entails identifying your assets, deciding who should inherit them, and drafting legal documents to ensure your wishes are carried out. Setting up a power of attorney, establishing a trust and successor trustees, or creating a living will are all examples of estate planning.

"Estate planning is not a one-time event; it's a lifelong process of adapting and aligning your assets and goals to create a lasting impact." - Unknown

Types of Assets

Assets can include a wide range of possessions, from financial accounts and real estate to personal belongings and digital assets. It's important to take stock of all your assets when creating an estate plan to ensure that everything is accounted for and distributed according to your wishes.

When drafting an estate plan, it is essential to consider various types of assets that you own or control. Here are some common types of assets that should be considered:

1. **Real Estate:** This includes any property you own, such as a primary residence, vacation home, rental

properties, land, or commercial real estate.

2. **Financial Assets:** These include cash, bank accounts, certificates of deposit (CDs), stocks, bonds, mutual funds, retirement accounts (e.g., IRAs, 401(k)s), annuities, and any other investment accounts.

3. **Business Interests:** If you own a business, whether it's a sole proprietorship, partnership, or corporation, it is crucial to determine how those interests will be managed, transferred, or sold upon your death.

4. **Personal Property:** This category encompasses tangible items such as vehicles, jewelry, artwork, furniture, collectibles, antiques, electronics, and any other possessions of value.

5. **Digital Assets:** In the digital age, it is essential to consider your online presence and digital assets, including email accounts, social media profiles, websites or blogs you own, digital photos, videos, and online financial accounts.

6. **Intellectual Property:** If you hold patents, trademarks, copyrights, or royalties from creative works, it is important to address how these assets will be managed and passed on.

7. **Life Insurance:** The proceeds from life insurance policies should be considered as part of your estate

plan, particularly if you want to provide financial support for your loved ones or cover estate taxes and expenses.

8. **Debts and Liabilities:** Estate planning involves not only determining how assets will be distributed but also addressing any outstanding debts, loans, mortgages, or other financial obligations.

In preparing an estate plan, it is crucial to provide detailed information about each asset, including its value, ownership structure, and any specific instructions for its distribution or management in your estate plan.

Tax Implications

Estate planning also includes thinking about the tax implications of transferring assets to heirs. Your estate may be subject to federal and state estate taxes, depending on the size of your estate and the state in which you live. There are, however, strategies you can employ to reduce these taxes and ensure that your assets are distributed as you intended. A well-crafted estate plan will take into account various tax implications and issues to ensure that your assets are transferred efficiently and effectively. The following are some important tax considerations in estate planning:

1. **Estate Tax:** Estate tax, also known as inheritance

tax or death tax, is a tax imposed on the transfer of an individual's assets upon their death. The tax is based on the total value of the estate and is subject to certain exemptions and thresholds set by the jurisdiction. Proper estate planning can help minimize estate tax liabilities through strategies such as gifting, establishing trusts, or leveraging marital deduction provisions.

2. **Gift Tax:** Gift tax is imposed on the transfer of assets during a person's lifetime. It applies when you give a substantial amount of money or property to someone else without receiving fair market value in return. There are annual and lifetime exemptions, which can be used strategically to transfer assets tax-free. Utilizing gifting strategies can help reduce the overall estate tax burden.

3. **Generation-Skipping Transfer Tax (GSTT):** The GSTT is a tax imposed on assets transferred to beneficiaries who are at least two generations younger than the transferor, such as grandchildren. It is an additional tax on top of estate and gift taxes. Proper estate planning can help minimize the impact of the GSTT by utilizing exemption amounts and establishing specific types of trusts, such as generation-skipping trusts.

4. **Capital Gains Tax:** Capital gains tax is applicable when an asset is sold or transferred and there is a gain in value. Upon the transfer of assets at death,

the assets receive a step-up in basis, which means the new cost basis becomes the fair market value at the time of death. This step-up in basis can minimize capital gains tax liabilities for the beneficiaries when they sell the inherited assets.

5. **Income Tax:** Income tax implications should be considered, especially for assets that generate income, such as rental properties, investment accounts, or retirement accounts. Different tax rules apply to different types of income, and proper planning can help optimize income tax efficiency for both the estate and beneficiaries.

6. **State Taxes:** In addition to federal taxes, state taxes may apply, including state estate taxes or inheritance taxes. Each state has its own laws and exemptions, so it's important to consider the specific tax implications in your jurisdiction.

Proper estate planning can involve utilizing various strategies, such as establishing trusts, creating charitable entities, utilizing exemptions, and coordinating beneficiary designations, to minimize tax liabilities and maximize the transfer of wealth to intended beneficiaries.

Legal Documents

Several key legal documents are typically included in

an estate plan. Here are some of the most common estate planning documents.

1. **Last Will and Testament:** A Last Will and Testament, often referred to as a will, is a legal document that outlines how a person's assets and properties should be distributed after their death. It allows individuals to specify beneficiaries, name guardians for minor children, appoint an executor to carry out their wishes and address other important matters such as funeral and burial preferences.

2. **Revocable Living Trust:** A revocable living trust is a legal entity created during an individual's lifetime to hold and manage their assets. The person creating the trust, known as the grantor or settlor, typically serves as the initial trustee. The trust provides instructions for the management and distribution of assets during the grantor's lifetime and upon their death. A revocable living trust helps avoid probate, provides privacy, and offers flexibility in managing assets.

3. **Durable Power of Attorney:** A durable power of attorney is a legal document that grants authority to a designated person (known as the attorney-in-fact or agent) to act on behalf of the individual (the principal) in making financial, legal, or other important decisions. This document remains in effect even if the principal becomes incapacitated.

4. **Healthcare Power of Attorney:** A healthcare power of attorney, also known as a healthcare proxy or medical power of attorney, designates an individual to make medical decisions on behalf of another person if they become unable to do so themselves. This document ensures that the individual's healthcare preferences and treatment decisions are respected.

5. **Living Will:** A living will is a legal document that expresses an individual's preferences regarding medical treatment and end-of-life care in the event they are unable to communicate their wishes. It typically covers decisions related to life-sustaining treatments, resuscitation, and organ donation.

6. **Beneficiary Designations:** Beneficiary designations are not legal documents themselves but are forms that individuals complete to designate beneficiaries for certain assets such as retirement accounts, life insurance policies, and payable-on-death (POD) or transfer-on-death (TOD) accounts. These designations dictate how these assets will be distributed upon the owner's death, bypassing probate.

7. **Letter of Intent:** A letter of intent is a non-binding document that outlines an individual's wishes, instructions, and preferences regarding the distribution of assets, succession planning, and other matters. While not a legally enforceable document, it guides family members and executors.

8. **Trust Documents:** In addition to revocable living trusts, various types of trusts may be used in estate planning, including irrevocable trusts, special needs trusts, charitable trusts, and more. Trust documents outline the terms and conditions under which the trust operates, including the beneficiaries, trustee responsibilities, distribution rules, and specific instructions for asset management.

These are some of the common legal documents involved in estate planning. The specific documents needed may vary based on individual circumstances and goals. Working with an experienced estate planning attorney is crucial to ensure that the appropriate documents are tailored to your specific needs and comply with relevant laws and regulations.

Conclusion

Estate planning can be a complex and emotional process, but it's essential to ensure that your assets are distributed according to your wishes and that your loved ones are taken care of after you pass away. In the next chapter, we'll dive into asset protection strategies and how you can protect your assets from creditors and other threats.

Chapter Two: **Protecting Your Assets**

Introduction

Asset protection is a critical aspect of estate planning, especially for high-net-worth individuals who have substantial assets to protect. In this chapter, we'll explore the different asset protection strategies you can use to safeguard your wealth and ensure that your beneficiaries receive the assets you intend them to.

Illustration

Let's consider the case of Carlos, a successful entrepreneur who has built a multi-million-dollar business empire over the years. Carlos has significant personal and business assets, including real estate properties, investments, and valuable intellectual property. He has worked tirelessly to accumulate wealth and wants to ensure its preservation and protection for his family and future generations.

One day, Carlos faces a lawsuit from a disgruntled business partner who claims a breach of contract and seeks substantial damages. Without an effective asset protection plan in place, all of Carlos's assets are at risk of being seized or heavily encumbered *to satisfy the judgment.*

However, because Carlos had the foresight to work with an experienced estate planning attorney to develop a comprehensive asset protection strategy, his assets are shielded to a significant extent. Through the use of legal structures such as trusts, limited liability companies (LLCs), and family limited partnerships (FLPs), Carlos has established layers of protection around his assets.

As a result, when the lawsuit occurs, only the assets held within the specific business entity involved in the dispute are exposed. The rest of Carlos's assets, held in separate entities or protected by specific legal structures, remain insulated from the lawsuit. This allows him to safeguard the majority of his wealth for the benefit of his family and future generations.

Furthermore, Carlos's asset protection plan includes provisions that limit his personal liability and protect his assets from other potential threats, such as creditor claims, bankruptcy, or divorce. By proactively implementing strategies like domestic asset protection trusts (DAPTs) or offshore trusts, Carlos has additional layers of protection in place to safeguard his wealth from unforeseen events or risks.

In this illustration, Carlos's experience demonstrates the importance of asset protection for high-net-worth individuals. Without a well-designed and implemented estate plan focused on asset protection, individuals like Carlos would be exposed to substantial risks that could jeopardize their wealth and financial security.

By working closely with knowledgeable professionals and implementing various legal tools and strategies, high-net-worth individuals can shield their assets from potential threats, litigation, and other risks. A robust asset protection plan helps ensure the preservation of wealth, maintains privacy, and provides a solid foundation for generational wealth transfer.

Asset Protection Strategies

There are several different asset protection strategies you can use to shield your assets from creditors and other threats. These include:

1. **Insurance:** Insurance policies, such as life insurance and liability insurance, can help protect your assets by providing a financial safety net in case of unexpected events.

2. **Trusts:** Trusts can be used to protect your assets by transferring ownership of them to a trustee. This can help shield them from creditors and legal judgments.

3. **Limited Liability Companies (LLCs):** Creating an LLC can help protect your personal assets from lawsuits and creditors by separating them from your business assets.

4. **Homestead Exemption:** Homestead exemptions can

protect your primary residence by shielding it from creditors and lawsuits up to a certain amount.

5. **Offshore Trusts:** Offshore trusts can offer additional protection for your assets by placing them outside the reach of U.S. creditors and legal judgments.

Choosing the Right Strategy

Choosing the right asset protection strategy depends on several factors, such as the size of your estate, your risk tolerance, and the type of assets you own. It's important to consult with a financial advisor or attorney to determine which strategy is best for your situation.

Conclusion

Protecting your assets is an essential part of estate planning, and there are several different strategies you can use to safeguard your wealth. In the next chapter, we'll dive into the importance of succession planning and how to ensure a smooth transfer of your assets to your heirs.

Chapter Three: **Succession Planning**

Introduction

Succession planning is the process of identifying and preparing the next generation of leaders and owners for a business or organization. For high-net-worth individuals, succession planning is essential to ensure a smooth transfer of assets to their heirs and to maintain their family legacy. In this chapter, we'll discuss the importance of succession planning and provide an overview of the key strategies involved.

Illustration

Meet Soliel, a successful business owner who has built a thriving company over the years. Her business has a loyal customer base, valuable intellectual property, and a dedicated team of employees. Soliel understands that her business is not only a significant source of income but also an essential part of her legacy.

One day, Soliel unexpectedly passes away due to a sudden illness. Without a proper succession plan in place, the future of her business becomes uncertain, causing disruption and potential loss for her employees, clients, and stakeholders.

However, because Soliel had the foresight to integrate a succession plan into her overall estate plan, the transition of her business is carefully orchestrated and minimizes any negative impact. The succession plan outlines a clear roadmap for the transfer of ownership and management of the business to a successor, ensuring continuity and preserving the value Soliel has built.

Soliel had identified a capable and trusted individual within her organization, Emily, as her chosen successor. With the help of legal and business advisors, Soliel prepared Emily for this role by providing mentorship, training, and gradual delegation of responsibilities over time. Emily was well-prepared to step into Soliel's shoes and lead the company effectively.

Soliel's succession plan also addressed key aspects such as ownership transfer, valuing the business, and ensuring a smooth transition of decision-making authority. It included provisions to handle potential conflicts among family members, existing partners, or shareholders, ensuring a fair and equitable distribution of shares and responsibilities.

By integrating her succession plan into her estate plan, Soliel also considered the financial aspects of the transition. She had implemented strategies such as life insurance policies, buy-sell agreements, or funding mechanisms to provide liquidity for the transfer of ownership, ensuring the business can continue operating without undue financial strain.

In this illustration, Soliel's experience demonstrates the importance of having a well-thought-out succession plan for entrepreneurs and business owners. Without a proper plan in place, the future of a business can be uncertain, leading to potential disruption, conflicts, and even the decline or dissolution of the business.

By incorporating a succession plan within her estate plan, Soliel ensured the smooth transition of her business to her chosen successor, preserving her legacy, protecting her employees' jobs, and securing the ongoing success of her business. This allowed her vision and hard work to continue impacting the lives of her employees, customers, and the community.

Entrepreneurs and business owners should recognize the significance of a succession plan and work with legal and business professionals to develop a comprehensive plan tailored to their specific needs and goals. By doing so, they can safeguard their business, maintain stability, and create a solid foundation for continued success beyond their lifetime.

Why Succession Planning Matters

Succession planning is crucial for several reasons. It ensures that the business or organization can continue to operate successfully after the current leaders retire or pass away. It also helps to maintain family harmony by reducing conflicts over the transfer of assets. Finally, succession planning allows for a more strategic and deliberate approach to managing the transfer of assets.

Key Strategies for Succession Planning

There are several key strategies involved in succession planning, including:

1. **Identifying potential successors:** Identifying potential successors is the first step in succession planning. This involves evaluating the skills and capabilities of family members or key employees who may be suitable candidates for leadership or ownership roles.

2. **Developing a plan:** Developing a succession plan involves creating a clear roadmap for how the transfer of assets will occur. This includes identifying the roles and responsibilities of each successor, as well as creating a timeline for the transfer of assets.

3. **Establishing clear communication:** Clear communication is essential to ensure that everyone involved in the succession planning process is on the same page. This involves communicating the plan to all stakeholders, including family members, employees, and advisors.

4. **Implementing the plan:** Implementing the plan involves putting the plan into action and ensuring that all necessary steps are taken to transfer assets to the next generation.

Challenges and Considerations

Succession planning can be a complex process, and there are several challenges and considerations to keep in mind. These include family dynamics, tax implications, and legal requirements. It's important to work with a team of advisors, including attorneys, financial planners, and accountants, to ensure that all aspects of the succession plan are addressed.

Conclusion

Succession planning is a critical component of estate planning, especially for high-net-worth individuals who want to ensure a smooth transfer of assets to their heirs. By following the key strategies and considerations outlined in this chapter, you can create a successful succession plan that maintains your family legacy and ensures the long-term success of your business or organization. In the next chapter, we'll discuss the importance of trusts in estate planning and how they can help protect your assets and ensure their proper distribution.

Chapter Four: **Trusts in Estate Planning**

Introduction

Trusts are powerful tools in estate planning that can help protect your assets, minimize taxes, and ensure the proper distribution of your wealth. In this chapter, we'll discuss the basics of trusts and the different types of trusts that are commonly used in estate planning.

Illustration

Meet James, a high-net-worth individual who has accumulated significant wealth through various investments, real estate holdings, and business ventures. James wants to ensure that his assets are protected, taxes are minimized, and his wealth is distributed according to his wishes while avoiding probate.

James decides to establish a revocable living trust as part of his estate planning strategy. By transferring his assets into the trust during his lifetime, James retains control over the assets as the trustee while designating beneficiaries to inherit them upon his passing.

Asset Protection: One of the primary benefits of the trust is asset protection. As the assets are held within the trust, they are shielded from potential creditors or legal claims. This can provide a layer of protection, especially for individuals in professions or industries with higher liability risks.

Minimizing Taxes: The trust also offers opportunities for minimizing taxes. James works closely with his estate planning attorney and financial advisor to structure the trust in a tax-efficient manner. They explore strategies such as gifting assets to the trust, utilizing exemptions and deductions, and leveraging trust provisions to optimize tax planning. By employing these strategies, James can potentially reduce estate taxes, income taxes, and capital gains taxes.

Probate Avoidance: By placing assets in a revocable living trust, James can avoid the probate process. Upon his passing, the assets held in the trust can be smoothly and privately transferred to the named beneficiaries, bypassing the need for court involvement. This helps to expedite the distribution of assets, maintain privacy, and potentially reduce administrative expenses.

Control and Flexibility: As the trustee of his revocable living trust, James maintains control over the trust assets during his lifetime. He has the flexibility to amend or revoke the trust, add or remove beneficiaries, and make changes as his circumstances evolve. This control allows James to adapt his estate plan to reflect his changing financial goals, family dynamics, or other considerations.

Wealth Distribution: James's revocable living trust provides clear instructions for the distribution of assets to his beneficiaries upon his passing. He can specify how and when the assets should be distributed, ensuring that his wealth is passed on according to his wishes. This allows for a more organized and efficient transfer of assets, avoiding potential conflicts or ambiguities that may arise in the absence of clear instructions.

In this illustration, James's experience showcases how a trust can be a valuable tool in protecting assets, minimizing taxes, and distributing wealth. By establishing trust and working with experienced professionals, individuals like James can take advantage of the benefits offered by trusts to ensure their assets are safeguarded, taxes are optimized, and their wealth is distributed in a controlled and efficient manner.

It's important to note that the specific strategies and benefits associated with trusts may vary depending on individual circumstances and applicable laws. It is crucial to consult with a qualified estate planning attorney and financial advisor to tailor the trust structure to one's unique needs and goals.

What is a Trust?

A trust is a legal arrangement in which a trustee holds and manages assets for the benefit of one or more beneficiaries. The trustee has a fiduciary duty to manage the assets in the best interests of the beneficiaries, and the beneficiaries have a right to the income and/or principal of the trust as specified in the trust agreement.

Types of Trusts

Several types of trusts are commonly used in estate planning, including:

1. **Revocable Trusts:** A revocable trust, also known as a living trust, is a trust that can be changed or revoked by the grantor during their lifetime. Revocable trusts are often used to avoid probate and to provide for the management of assets in the event of incapacity.

2. **Irrevocable Trusts:** An irrevocable trust is a trust that cannot be changed or revoked by the grantor once it's established. Irrevocable trusts are often used for tax planning purposes, as assets transferred to an irrevocable trust are generally no longer subject to estate taxes.

3. **Testamentary Trusts:** A testamentary trust is a trust that is established in a will and only takes effect upon the grantor's death. Testamentary trusts are often used to provide for minor children or beneficiaries with special needs.

4. **Charitable Trusts:** A charitable trust is a trust that is established for charitable purposes. Charitable trusts can provide tax benefits and allow the grantor to support causes they care about.

Benefits of Trusts

There are several benefits of using trusts in estate planning, including:

1. **Asset protection:** Trusts can help protect your assets from creditors and lawsuits.

2. **Tax planning:** Trusts can help minimize estate and gift taxes, as well as income taxes in some cases.

3. **Control over asset distribution:** Trusts allow you to specify how and when your assets will be distributed to your beneficiaries.

4. **Privacy:** Trusts can be used to avoid the public probate process, which can be time-consuming and expensive.

Conclusion

Trusts are a powerful tool in estate planning that can help protect your assets, minimize taxes, and ensure the proper distribution of your wealth. By working with a team of advisors, including attorneys and financial planners, you can create a trust that meets your specific needs and goals. In the next chapter, we'll discuss the importance of regularly reviewing and updating your estate plan to ensure that it reflects your current wishes and circumstances.

Chapter Five: **The Importance of Regularly Reviewing and Updating Your Estate Plan**

Introduction

Estate planning is not a one-time event, but rather an ongoing process that requires regular review and updating. In this chapter, we'll discuss the importance of regularly reviewing and updating your estate plan to ensure that it reflects your current wishes and circumstances.

Illustration

Meet Laura, a successful businesswoman who diligently created her estate plan several years ago. Her estate plan included a will, trust, power of attorney, and healthcare directives, all designed to protect her assets, provide for her loved ones, and ensure her healthcare wishes are followed.

Over the years, Laura's circumstances have changed significantly. She sold her business, acquired new assets, and experienced important life events such as marriage, the birth of children, and the passing of loved ones. However, Laura neglected to review and update her estate plan to reflect these changes.

One day, Laura suddenly falls ill and becomes incapacitated. Her family discovers that her estate plan does not account for her new assets, her recent marriage, or the arrival of her newborn child. The lack of updates and revisions in her estate plan creates confusion, uncertainty, and potential conflicts among her family members.

If Laura had regularly updated her estate plan, she could have ensured that her wishes and intentions were accurately reflected. By keeping her plan current, Laura could have:

1. *Included her new assets: Updating her estate plan would have allowed Laura to incorporate her newly acquired assets, ensuring they are properly accounted for and distributed according to her wishes.*

2. *Reflected changes in marital status: Laura's recent marriage should have been addressed in her estate plan to protect the rights and interests of her spouse, clarify inheritance provisions, and potentially establish appropriate trusts or beneficiary designations.*

3. *Provided for her newborn child: By updating her estate plan, Laura could have designated a guardian for her child, established a trust to manage the child's inheritance, and put in place provisions to ensure the child's financial well-being and upbringing.*

4. *Reviewed and adjusted beneficiary designations: Regularly reviewing and updating beneficiary designations on financial accounts, life insurance policies, retirement*

plans, and other assets is crucial to ensure they align with the intended distribution of assets in the estate plan.

5. Addressed changes in healthcare directives: Laura's healthcare directives may need updating to reflect any changes in her healthcare preferences or to designate a trusted individual to make medical decisions on her behalf.

By neglecting to regularly update her estate plan, Laura's intentions and desires were not accurately represented during her incapacitation. This situation resulted in unnecessary confusion, potential legal disputes, and delays in making important decisions on her behalf.

This illustration emphasizes the importance of regularly reviewing and updating your estate plan. Life events, financial changes, family dynamics, and legal developments can significantly impact the effectiveness and relevance of your estate plan over time. By proactively reviewing and making necessary updates, you can ensure that your plan remains current, aligned with your wishes, and capable of addressing your evolving needs and circumstances.

It's advisable to consult with an experienced estate planning attorney who can guide you through the process of updating your estate plan, provide personalized advice, and ensure that your plan reflects your current goals and priorities.

Why Regular Review and Updating are Necessary

There are several reasons why regularly reviewing and updating your estate plan is important, including:

1. **Changes in Your Family and Financial Situation:** Your family and financial situation may change over time, such as the birth of a child, a divorce, or a significant change in your assets. These changes may require updates to your estate plan to ensure that your wishes are still being met.

2. **Changes in the Law:** Tax laws and other legal regulations may change over time, which could impact your estate plan. Regular review and updating can help ensure that your plan remains compliant with current laws.

3. **Changes in Your Goals and Wishes:** Your goals and wishes for your estate may change over time, such as a desire to support a different charity or to change the distribution of your assets. Regular review and updating can help ensure that your estate plan reflects your current wishes and priorities.

When to Review and Update Your Estate Plan

While there is no set schedule for reviewing and updating your estate plan, there are certain life events and milestones that should prompt a review, including:

1. **Marriage, Divorce, or Remarriage:** Any changes to your marital status should prompt a review of your estate plan.

2. **2. Birth or Adoption of a Child:** The addition of a child to your family should prompt a review of your estate plan to ensure that the child is properly provided for.

3. **3. Death of a Beneficiary or Executor:** The death of a beneficiary or executor named in your estate plan should prompt a review to ensure that alternate arrangements are in place.

4. **4. Significant Changes in Assets:** Significant changes in your assets, such as the acquisition or sale of a business, should prompt a review of your estate plan.

Conclusion

Regularly reviewing and updating your estate plan is a critical part of ensuring that your wishes are carried out and your loved ones are properly provided for. By working with a team of advisors, including attorneys and financial planners, you can create an estate plan that reflects your current wishes and circumstances and provides peace of mind for you and your family. In the next chapter, we'll discuss some common mistakes to avoid when creating an estate plan.

Chapter Six: Common Estate Planning Mistakes and How to Avoid Them

Introduction

While creating an estate plan is crucial for leaving a financial legacy for your loved ones, there are many common mistakes that people make during the process. In this chapter, we'll discuss some of the most common estate planning mistakes and how to avoid them.

Mistake #1: Not Having an Estate Plan

One of the biggest mistakes that people make is not having an estate plan at all. Without a plan, your assets may not be distributed according to your wishes, and your loved ones may not receive the support they need. To avoid this mistake, it's important to work with an attorney to create a comprehensive estate plan that reflects your goals and priorities.

Mistake #2: Failing to Update Your Estate Plan

As discussed in the previous chapter, failing to update your estate plan regularly is another common mistake. If your plan is not updated to reflect changes in your family or financial situation, it may not accurately reflect your wishes and may not provide the necessary support for your loved ones. To avoid this mistake, it's important to review and update your estate plan regularly, especially after major life events.

Mistake #3: Not Considering Taxes

Another common mistake is not considering the tax implications of your estate plan. Estate taxes can have a significant impact on the value of your assets, and failing to plan for them can result in unnecessary taxes and fees. To avoid this mistake, it's important to work with a financial planner and an attorney who can help you create a plan that minimizes taxes and maximizes the value of your estate.

Mistake #4: Failing to Plan for Incapacity

While most people focus on distributing their assets after their death, it's important to also plan for incapacity. If you become unable to make decisions for yourself due to illness or injury, a plan for incapacity can ensure that your wishes are still carried out and that your loved ones are properly cared for. To avoid this mistake, it's important to work with an attorney to create a power of attorney and healthcare directive that reflects your wishes.

Mistake #5: Not Communicating with Your Loved Ones

Finally, a common mistake is failing to communicate with your loved ones about your estate plan. If your loved ones are not aware of your wishes or the details of your plan, it can create confusion and conflict after your death. To avoid this mistake, it's important to communicate with your loved ones about your wishes and the details of your plan and to consider including them in the planning process if appropriate.

Conclusion

Creating an estate plan is a critical part of leaving a financial legacy for your loved ones, but it's important to avoid common mistakes that can compromise your plan. By working with an attorney and other advisors, and by regularly reviewing and updating your plan, you can create a plan that reflects your wishes and provides the necessary support for your loved ones. In the final chapter, we'll discuss some tips for choosing the right advisors for your estate planning needs.

Chapter Seven: Choosing the Right Advisors for Your Estate Planning Needs

Introduction

Creating an estate plan is a complex process that requires input from a variety of professionals. In this chapter, we'll discuss the key advisors you may need to work with to create an effective estate plan and provide some tips for choosing the right ones for your needs.

Illustration

Meet Oscar, a successful entrepreneur who has accumulated substantial wealth over the years. He understands the importance of proper estate planning and wants to ensure that his assets are protected, his family is taken care of, and his wishes are fulfilled.

Oscar realizes that navigating the complexities of estate planning requires expertise and guidance from professionals. He decides to assemble a team of advisors to assist him in creating a comprehensive estate plan that aligns with his goals.

1. Estate Planning Attorney: Oscar carefully selects an experienced estate planning attorney who specializes in working with high-net-worth individuals. The attorney helps Oscar understand the legal implications of various estate planning strategies and assists him in drafting the necessary legal documents such as wills, trusts, and powers of attorney. The attorney ensures that Oscar's estate plan is tailored to his specific needs, considers tax implications, and complies with applicable laws.

2. Financial Advisor: Recognizing the financial intricacies involved in estate planning, Oscar engages a qualified financial advisor. The financial advisor analyzes Oscar's assets, investments, and retirement accounts to develop a comprehensive financial strategy that aligns with his estate planning objectives. They assess potential tax implications, investment strategies, and long-term financial goals to optimize Oscar's wealth preservation and distribution plans.

3. Accountant or Tax Professional: Oscar understands the importance of tax efficiency in estate planning. He consults with an accountant or tax professional who is knowledgeable about estate and gift tax laws. The tax professional guides strategies to minimize tax liabilities, take advantage of exemptions and deductions, and navigate complex tax regulations. They work closely with Oscar's estate planning attorney and financial advisor to ensure a cohesive approach.

4. Trustee or Fiduciary: Oscar considers designating a trustee or fiduciary to manage his assets and carry out his wishes in the event of his incapacitation or passing. He carefully selects an individual or institution that is trustworthy, reliable, and experienced in administering trusts. The trustee ensures that the assets are distributed according to Oscar's instructions, handles any legal or financial matters, and acts in the best interests of his beneficiaries.

5. Family Counselor or Mediator: Recognizing the potential for emotional complexities and family dynamics in estate planning, Oscar engages a family counselor or mediator. This professional helps facilitate open and honest communication among family members, ensuring that everyone's concerns are heard and addressed. They assist in resolving conflicts, promoting understanding, and fosteringg a harmonious environment to maintain family relationships during the estate planning process.

By carefully selecting the right advisors, Oscar can benefit from their expertise, knowledge, and experience in their respective fields. They provide him with comprehensive guidance, collaborate to create a cohesive estate plan and help navigate potential challenges along the way. The collective wisdom of his advisors ensures that Oscar's estate plan is robust, legally sound, tax-efficient, and aligned with his wishes and goals.

Choosing the right advisors for estate planning is crucial in developing a comprehensive plan that addresses legal, financial, and emotional aspects. It allows individuals like Oscar to have peace of mind, knowing that they have a trusted team of professionals who are committed to their best interests and the long-term success of their estate plan.

Financial Planner

A financial planner can be an important advisor in the estate planning process, especially when it comes to minimizing taxes and maximizing the value of your estate. A financial planner can also help you assess your financial situation, set goals for your estate plan, and create a plan for managing your assets during your lifetime.

Estate Planning Attorney

An estate planning attorney is a critical advisor in the estate planning process, as they can help you create a comprehensive estate plan that reflects your goals and priorities. An attorney can also help you navigate complex legal issues related to estate planning, such as taxes, probate, and trust administration.

Accountant

An accountant can be an important advisor in the estate planning process, especially when it comes to taxes. An accountant can help you understand the tax implications of your estate plan, and provide advice on how to minimize taxes and maximize the value of your estate.

Insurance Agent

An insurance agent can be an important advisor in the estate planning process, especially when it comes to life insurance. Life insurance can be an effective tool for providing for your loved ones after your death, and an insurance agent can help you assess your insurance needs and choose the right policy for your situation.

Trust Officer

If you are creating a trust as part of your estate plan, a trust officer can be an important advisor. A trust officer can help you choose the right type of trust for your needs, and provide guidance on trust administration and management.

Tips for Choosing the Right Advisors

When choosing advisors for your estate planning needs, it's important to do your research and choose professionals who are experienced, knowledgeable, and trustworthy. Here are some tips to help you choose the right advisors:

- Ask for referrals from friends, family, and other professionals.

- Check credentials and professional affiliations.

- Consider experience and expertise in estate planning.

- Look for advisors who are transparent about their fees and costs.

- Choose advisors who are responsive and communicative.

Conclusion

Choosing the right advisors is critical to creating an effective estate plan that reflects your wishes and provides the necessary support for your loved ones. By working with experienced and knowledgeable professionals, doing your research, and asking the right questions, you can create a team of advisors who can help you navigate the complex process of estate planning. In the final chapter, we'll provide some additional tips and resources for creating an effective estate plan.

Chapter Eight: Putting Your Estate Plan Into Action

Introduction

Now that you've worked with your advisors to create an estate plan that reflects your goals and priorities, it's time to put that plan into action. In this chapter, we'll discuss the key steps you'll need to take to implement your estate plan and ensure that your wishes are carried out after your death.

Illustration

Meet Jennifer, a successful businesswoman who has diligently worked on her estate plan for many years. She has taken the necessary steps to protect her assets, minimize taxes, and ensure a smooth transfer of wealth to her loved ones. Let's take a look at how Jennifer's estate plan has been successfully implemented:

1. *Asset Protection: Jennifer worked closely with her estate planning attorney to establish a comprehensive asset protection plan. By utilizing a combination of trusts, business entities, and insurance policies, Jennifer has safeguarded her assets from potential creditors and legal claims. This strategic approach has provided her with*

peace of mind, knowing that her hard-earned assets are shielded and preserved for the benefit of her beneficiaries.

2. *Tax Optimization: Jennifer's estate plan incorporates various tax optimization strategies. She has utilized gift and estate tax exemptions, implemented tax-efficient gifting strategies, and established charitable giving plans to reduce her overall tax liabilities. By working closely with her estate planning team, Jennifer has successfully minimized the impact of estate and gift taxes, allowing more of her wealth to be passed on to her intended beneficiaries.*

3. *Business Succession: Jennifer is a business owner and understands the importance of succession planning. As part of her estate plan, she has developed a detailed succession plan for her business. This plan outlines the transition of ownership and management to a designated successor, ensuring the continuity of the business and the preservation of its value. By carefully selecting and preparing her successor, Jennifer has set the stage for a smooth transfer of business assets and responsibilities.*

4. *Beneficiary Designations: Jennifer regularly reviews and updates the beneficiary designations on her retirement accounts, life insurance policies, and other financial assets. This ensures that her assets are distributed according to her wishes, and it avoids potential complications or disputes that can arise if beneficiary designations are outdated or inconsistent with her overall estate plan.*

5. *Communication with Family: Jennifer believes in open*

and transparent communication with her family about her estate plan. She has taken the time to discuss her wishes, intentions, and the roles and responsibilities of various family members involved in the estate plan. By engaging in Jennifer has fostered a sense of unity and understanding among her loved ones through these conversations and addressing any questions or concerns, reducing potential conflicts and ensuring a smoother implementation of her estate plan.

Jennifer's estate plan was successfully implemented thanks to careful planning, regular updates, and effective communication. Her assets are safeguarded, taxes are reduced, business succession is planned, and her beneficiaries are fully aware of her wishes. As a result, Jennifer can relax knowing that her estate plan will be carried out smoothly, ensuring the financial security and well-being of her loved ones.

It's important to note that the successful implementation of an estate plan may vary depending on individual circumstances, applicable laws, and ongoing management. Working closely with experienced professionals, such as estate planning attorneys, financial advisors, and tax experts, is crucial in ensuring the effective execution of an estate plan tailored to one's unique goals and needs.

Review Your Estate Plan Regularly

Your estate plan is not a static document, and it's important to review and update it regularly to ensure that it still reflects your wishes and priorities. Changes in your family situation, financial situation, or the law can all impact your estate plan, so it's important to review it every few years or after major life events.

Communicate Your Wishes to Your Family and Loved Ones

One of the most important steps you can take to ensure that your estate plan is carried out as intended is to communicate your wishes to your family and loved ones. This can help prevent misunderstandings or disputes after your death and can provide your loved ones with the guidance and support they need during a difficult time.

Update Beneficiary Designations and Titles

In addition to updating your estate plan regularly, it's important to ensure that your beneficiary designations and titles are up-to-date and consistent with your estate plan. For example, if you create a trust as part of your estate plan, you'll need to ensure that your assets are properly titled in the name of the trust.

Consider Life Insurance and Long-Term Care Insurance

Life insurance and long-term care insurance can be effective tools for protecting your loved ones and preserving your assets. Consider whether these types of insurance may be appropriate for your situation, and work with your insurance agent to choose the right policies for your needs.

Choose the Right Executor and Trustees

Your executor and trustees will play a critical role in carrying out your estate plan after your death. It's important to choose individuals who are trustworthy, reliable, and capable of managing the responsibilities of executor or trustee.

Conclusion

Putting your estate plan into action can be a difficult process, but by taking the necessary steps and collaborating with your advisors, you can ensure that your wishes are carried out as intended. You can create a comprehensive estate plan that provides for your loved ones and protects your legacy by reviewing and updating your estate plan on a regular basis, communicating your wishes to your loved ones, updating beneficiary designations and titles, considering life insurance and long-term care insurance, and selecting the right executor and trustees.

Chapter Nine: **Trusts for Legacy Planning**

Introduction

Trusts can be powerful tools for legacy planning, allowing you to control and protect your assets both during your lifetime and after your death. In this chapter, we'll discuss the different types of trusts that you can use to leave a financial legacy for your children, and how to choose the right trust for your situation.

Illustration

Meet the Zaldivar family, a multigenerational family with a diverse cultural background. They have accumulated significant wealth over the years and want to ensure that their legacy is preserved and distributed in a way that aligns with their values and addresses the unique dynamics of their family.

1. *Cultural Considerations: The Zaldivar family recognizes the importance of honoring their cultural heritage in their estate planning. They establish a trust that incorporates cultural traditions and values into their wealth distribution strategy. For example, they may include provisions in the trust that allocate funds for cultural celebrations,*

educational programs promoting their cultural heritage, or philanthropic efforts benefiting their ancestral community. By utilizing trust, the Zaldivar family can preserve and pass down their cultural legacy to future generations while promoting unity and understanding among family members.

2. *Racial Equity: The Zaldivar family is committed to promoting racial equity and addressing historical wealth disparities. They establish a charitable trust or a donor-advised fund within their estate plan to support organizations and initiatives that advance racial justice, economic empowerment, and educational opportunities for marginalized communities. The trust can be structured to provide ongoing support or allocate a percentage of their wealth to address racial disparities. Through trust, the Zaldivar family can leave a lasting impact on the broader community and contribute to a more equitable society.*

3. *Socioeconomic Dynamics: The Zaldivar family recognizes the socioeconomic dynamics within their family, with varying levels of financial resources among different members. They establish a trust that allows for the equitable distribution of assets while taking into account individual needs and circumstances. The trust may include provisions for discretionary distributions, educational support, or business opportunities tailored to specific family members' financial situations. By utilizing a trust, the Zaldivar family can ensure that their wealth is distributed in a manner that promotes fairness, opportunities, and long-term financial stability for all beneficiaries.*

4. *Education and Financial Literacy:* The Zaldivar family believes in empowering future generations with knowledge and skills to manage their wealth responsibly. They establish educational trusts or scholarships to support the academic pursuits of their descendants. Additionally, they incorporate financial literacy programs or resources within the trust, providing educational opportunities for family members to learn about wealth management, investment strategies, and responsible financial practices. Through these initiatives, the Zaldivar family can equip their heirs with the tools they need to navigate financial complexities and make informed decisions for their own financial well-being.

By utilizing trusts within their estate plan, the Zaldivar family can effectively incorporate cultural, racial, and socioeconomic dynamics into their legacy planning. Trusts provide the flexibility and customization necessary to address their unique considerations and ensure that their wealth distribution aligns with their values and promotes long-lasting positive impact within their family and the broader society.

It's important to note that each family's circumstances and values are unique, and the specific provisions and structures of trusts should be tailored to their individual needs. Consulting with experienced professionals, such as estate planning attorneys and financial advisors with expertise in cultural and socioeconomic dynamics, can provide valuable guidance in designing and implementing trusts that align with one's specific legacy planning goals.

Revocable Living Trusts

A revocable living trust is a type of trust that you can create during your lifetime and that you can modify or revoke at any time. One of the main benefits of a revocable living trust is that it can help you avoid probate, a potentially lengthy and costly court process that can tie up your assets for months or even years.

Irrevocable Trusts

An irrevocable trust is a type of trust that you cannot modify or revoke once it's created. One of the main benefits of an irrevocable trust is that it can provide significant tax benefits, both during your lifetime and after your death. For example, you can use an irrevocable life insurance trust (ILIT) to exclude the proceeds of a life insurance policy from your estate, reducing your estate tax liability.

Asset Protection Trusts

An asset protection trust is a type of trust that's designed to protect your assets from creditors, lawsuits, and other potential threats. Depending on the state in which you live, you may be able to create a domestic asset protection trust (DAPT) that can provide you with significant protection from creditors.

Special Needs Trusts

A special needs trust is a type of trust that's designed to provide for the needs of a person with a disability without jeopardizing their eligibility for government benefits. By creating a special needs trust, you can ensure that your loved one with special needs will be able to receive the care and support they need without losing access to government benefits like Medicaid or Supplemental Security Income (SSI).

Choosing the Right Trust for Your Needs

Choosing the right trust for your situation will depend on a variety of factors, including your goals, your assets, and your family situation. It's important to work with an experienced estate planning attorney to help you evaluate your options and choose the right trust for your needs.

Conclusion

Trusts can be powerful tools for leaving a financial legacy for your children and protecting your assets for future generations. By understanding the different types of trusts available, including revocable living trusts, irrevocable trusts, asset protection trusts, and special needs trusts, and by working with an experienced estate planning attorney, you can create a comprehensive legacy plan that provides for your loved ones and protects your assets for years to come.

Chapter Ten: **Administering Trusts and Estate Plans**

Introduction

Administering a trust or estate plan after the death of a loved one can be a complex and challenging process. In this chapter, we'll discuss the steps involved in administering a trust or estate plan, including how to handle estate taxes, distribute assets to beneficiaries, and fulfill any other wishes outlined in the trust or estate plan.

Estate Tax Returns

One of the first steps in administering a trust or estate plan is to file estate tax returns, both with the federal government and, if applicable, with the state in which the deceased lived. The estate tax return will provide a snapshot of the deceased's assets and liabilities and will determine whether any estate taxes are owed.

Paying Estate Taxes

If estate taxes are owed, it's important to pay them as soon as possible to avoid any penalties or interest. This may require liquidating some assets in the estate to generate cash to pay the taxes.

Distributing Assets to Beneficiaries

Once estate taxes and any other debts or expenses have been paid, the remaining assets can be distributed to beneficiaries according to the wishes outlined in the trust or estate plan. Depending on the nature of the assets and the terms of the trust or estate plan, this may involve selling assets, transferring assets to beneficiaries, or distributing assets in-kind.

Handling Contingencies and Unforeseen Circumstances

Even with a well-crafted estate plan, there may be contingencies or unforeseen circumstances that arise during the administration process. For example, a beneficiary may pass away before receiving their share of the estate, or there may be disputes among beneficiaries over the distribution of assets. It's important to work with an experienced estate planning attorney to help you navigate these situations and ensure that the estate plan is carried out per the deceased's wishes.

Closing the Trust or Estate

Once all the assets have been distributed and all the administrative tasks have been completed, the trust or estate can be closed. This typically involves filing final tax returns, distributing any remaining assets to beneficiaries, and obtaining releases from the beneficiaries acknowledging that they have received their share of the estate.

Conclusion

Administering a trust or estate plan can be a complex and challenging process, but with careful planning and the help of an experienced estate planning attorney, you can ensure that your loved ones are taken care of and that your wishes are carried out after your death. By understanding the steps involved in administering a trust or estate plan, including filing estate tax returns, distributing assets to beneficiaries, and handling contingencies and unforeseen circumstances, you can create a comprehensive plan that provides for your loved ones and protects your assets for years to come.

Chapter Eleven: Protecting Your Legacy Through Charitable Giving

Introduction

Charitable giving is a powerful way to leave a lasting legacy that benefits both your community and your family. In this chapter, we'll discuss the benefits of charitable giving, different ways to structure charitable gifts, and how to include charitable giving in your estate plan.

Illustration

Meet Estrella and George, a couple who strongly believes in giving back to their community and making a positive impact on the causes they care about. They have decided to incorporate charitable giving into their estate plan to ensure their philanthropic goals continue beyond their lifetime.

1. *Establishing a Donor-Advised Fund: Estrella and George decide to establish a donor-advised fund (DAF) as part of their estate plan. They contribute a significant portion of their wealth to the DAF during their lifetime, and the fund is set up to provide ongoing support to various charitable*

organizations. *By using a DAF, they can benefit from immediate tax advantages while retaining the flexibility to recommend grants to charitable organizations in the future. This allows them to involve their family in the philanthropic decision-making process and instill a sense of giving in future generations.*

2. *Creating a Charitable Trust: Estrella and George also establish a charitable remainder trust (CRT) as part of their estate plan. They transfer assets into the trust, which then generates income for them during their lifetime. After their passing, the remaining assets in the trust are directed to their chosen charitable organizations. This approach allows them to receive income tax benefits during their lifetime while ultimately leaving a substantial charitable legacy.*

3. *Designating Charitable Beneficiaries: Within their estate plan, Estrella and George name specific charitable organizations as beneficiaries of certain assets. For example, they may designate a portion of their retirement accounts or life insurance policies to go directly to their preferred charities. By including these designations, they ensure that their chosen organizations receive significant support upon their passing.*

4. *Charitable Bequests: Estrella and George also include charitable bequests in their wills. They allocate a portion of their estate to be distributed to their favorite charities upon their passing. This allows them to support causes they deeply care about and leave a lasting impact in the*

areas they consider most meaningful.

5. *Encouraging Family Philanthropy: Estrella and George involve their children and grandchildren in their charitable giving efforts. They hold regular family meetings to discuss the family's philanthropic goals, share information about the causes they support, and encourage the next generations to actively participate in charitable activities. By instilling a culture of giving within the family, Estrella and George ensure that their legacy of charitable giving continues to thrive for years to come.*

Through careful planning and the integration of charitable giving into their estate plan, Estrella and George establish a lasting legacy of philanthropy. Their estate plan allows them to support causes they are passionate about, involve their family in charitable decision-making, and make a meaningful impact in their community and beyond. By leveraging various estate planning tools and strategies, they ensure that their charitable intentions are carried out according to their wishes and leave a positive and enduring legacy.

It's important to consult with experienced professionals, such as estate planning attorneys and financial advisors with expertise in charitable giving, to navigate the complexities of incorporating philanthropy into an estate plan. They can provide guidance on the most suitable charitable giving vehicles, tax implications, and strategies to maximize the impact of charitable contributions.

Benefits of Charitable Giving

Charitable giving allows you to make a positive impact on the causes and organizations that you care about. In addition to the satisfaction of giving back, charitable giving can also provide tax benefits and help you leave a lasting legacy.

Types of Charitable Gifts

There are several ways to structure charitable gifts, each with its own benefits and considerations. Some common types of charitable gifts include:

- Cash Gifts: Donating cash to a charity is a straightforward way to give back.

- Appreciated Securities: Donating appreciated securities can provide significant tax benefits, including avoiding capital gains taxes.

- Charitable Remainder Trusts: A charitable remainder trust allows you to make a gift to a charity while also receiving income for yourself or your loved ones during your lifetime.

- Charitable Lead Trusts: A charitable lead trust allows you to make a gift to a charity while also passing assets to your loved ones.

Incorporating Charitable Giving into Your Estate Plan

Charitable giving can be incorporated into your estate plan in a variety of ways. You may choose to leave a specific dollar amount or percentage of your estate to a charity in your will or trust. Alternatively, you may establish a charitable trust during your lifetime that provides income to you or your loved ones while also benefitting a charity. Working with an experienced estate planning attorney can help you determine the best way to incorporate charitable giving into your estate plan.

Selecting Charities

Beyond the immediate family, an estate plan provides an opportunity to create a lasting legacy by supporting causes and organizations that hold a special place in your heart. Choosing which charities to support can be a personal and meaningful decision. It's important to research the charities you're considering to ensure that they align with your values and will use your gift effectively. There are several resources available, such as charity rating websites and online giving portals, that can help you make informed decisions about which charities to support.

For many people, their college or university holds cherished memories, shaped their education, and helped pave the way for their future success. Including planned giving to your alma mater in your estate plan allows you to leave a lasting impact on future generations of students. By designating a gift to your college or university, whether through a scholarship fund, an endowment, or a specific program, you can help create opportunities for aspiring students and contribute to the growth and development of the institution. Your estate plan becomes a testament to your commitment to education and ensures that your alma mater continues to thrive long after you are gone, leaving a lasting legacy that echoes your values and passion for learning.

Conclusion

Charitable giving is a powerful way to leave a lasting legacy that benefits both your community and your family. By understanding the benefits of charitable giving, the different ways to structure charitable gifts, and how to incorporate charitable giving into your estate plan, you can create a comprehensive plan that provides for your loved ones and supports the causes and organizations that you care about for generations to come.

Chapter Twelve: **Protecting Your Digital Assets and Digital Legacy**

Introduction

In today's digital age, many of our personal and financial assets are stored online, making it important to include digital assets in your estate plan. In this chapter, we'll discuss what digital assets are, why it's important to include them in your estate plan, and how to protect your digital legacy.

Illustration

Meet Erin, a tech-savvy businesswoman who has accumulated a significant number of digital assets over the years. These assets include digital files such as photos, videos, music, and documents, as well as online accounts, social media profiles, and cryptocurrencies. Erin wants to ensure that her digital assets are protected, managed and passed on to her loved ones according to her wishes.

1. *Digital Asset Inventory: Erin starts by creating an inventory of her digital assets. She compiles a comprehensive list of her online accounts, including email, social media, cloud storage, and financial platforms. She also identifies the*

types of digital assets she possesses, such as photos, videos, music libraries, and cryptocurrency holdings. This inventory will serve as a valuable reference for her estate planning and ensure that no digital assets are overlooked.

2. *Password Management: Erin understands the importance of secure password management. She uses a reputable password manager to store and organize her login credentials for various online accounts. She ensures that her executor or designated representative has access to the password manager or provides instructions on how to retrieve the necessary passwords in case of her incapacity or passing. This ensures that her loved ones can access and manage her digital assets appropriately.*

3. *Digital Estate Planning Document: Erin includes provisions for her digital assets within her estate planning documents. She specifically addresses the management, access, and distribution of her digital assets. For example, she may provide instructions on how her executor can access her digital accounts, retrieve important files, or close down accounts if necessary. Additionally, she may outline her preferences regarding the preservation, deletion, or transfer of specific digital assets to family members or other beneficiaries.*

4. *Online Service Providers' Policies: Erin familiarizes herself with the terms of service and policies of the online platforms she uses. Some platforms have specific procedures for handling digital assets upon a user's incapacity or passing. Erin takes note of these policies and ensures that her estate*

plan aligns with the platform's guidelines. She may need to designate certain individuals as authorized users or include specific instructions to comply with these policies.

5. *Digital Executor or Trusted Agent:* Erin designates a digital executor or trusted agent within her estate plan. This individual is responsible for managing her digital assets following her wishes. Erin selects someone tech-savvy and trustworthy to handle the complexities of her digital estate. She communicates her intentions and expectations regarding the handling of her digital assets to the designated individual, ensuring a smooth transition and protection of her digital legacy.

6. *Communication and Education:* Erin understands the importance of open communication with her loved ones regarding her digital assets and online presence. She discusses her wishes and the steps she has taken to protect and manage her digital legacy with her family members or designated beneficiaries. She may provide guidance on how to access and handle her digital assets, making sure they are aware of her intentions and any specific instructions she has included in her estate plan.

By incorporating strategies and provisions within her estate plan, Erin ensures that her digital assets and digital legacy are protected and managed effectively. Her estate plan provides guidance to her loved ones, facilitates access to her digital accounts, and ensures that her wishes regarding her digital assets are carried out.

It's important to consult with experienced professionals, such as estate planning attorneys and digital asset specialists, to navigate the complexities of protecting digital assets and incorporating a digital legacy into an estate plan. They can provide guidance on legal considerations, privacy concerns, and strategies for preserving and passing on digital assets according to individual preferences and applicable laws.

What are Digital Assets?

Digital assets include any electronic information that you own or have rights to, such as online bank accounts, social media accounts, email accounts, digital photos and videos, domain names, cryptocurrency, and more.

Why Include Digital Assets in Your Estate Plan?

Without a plan for your digital assets, your loved ones may have difficulty accessing or managing them after your death. Additionally, without proper planning, your digital legacy may be lost or mishandled.

Protecting Your Digital Legacy

There are several steps you can take to protect your digital legacy, including:

- Create an inventory of your digital assets: Make a list of all your digital assets, including usernames and passwords.

- Appoint a digital executor: Appoint someone you trust to manage your digital assets and digital legacy after your death.

- Include digital assets in your estate plan: Your estate plan should include provisions for how your digital assets will be managed and distributed after your death.

- Use secure passwords and two-factor authentication: Using strong passwords and two-factor authentication can help protect your digital assets from hackers.

- Consider online backup and storage options: Storing your digital assets in the cloud or using online backup services can help ensure that your digital legacy is preserved and accessible to your loved ones.

Conclusion

As our lives become increasingly digitized, it's important to include digital assets in your estate plan. By understanding what digital assets are, why it's important to include them in your estate plan, and how to protect your digital legacy, you can create a comprehensive plan that provides for your loved ones and ensures that your digital legacy is preserved for generations to come.

Chapter Thirteen: Conclusion - Leaving a Lasting Legacy

In this book, we've discussed the importance of estate and succession planning, and how it can help you leave a lasting legacy for your loved ones. From understanding the basics of estate planning to creating a business succession plan, we've covered a lot of ground.

Throughout the book, we've emphasized the importance of taking action and starting your estate planning process as soon as possible. By doing so, you can help ensure that your assets are distributed according to your wishes and that your family is taken care of in the event of your death.

We've also discussed the importance of working with professionals, such as attorneys, financial planners, and accountants, to create a comprehensive estate plan. These professionals can provide valuable guidance and expertise to help you make informed decisions about your estate and succession planning.

In addition to the technical aspects of estate planning, we've also discussed the emotional side of leaving a legacy. By considering what kind of legacy you want to leave and how you want to be remembered, you can create a plan that reflects your values and priorities.

Finally, we've discussed the importance of regularly reviewing and updating your estate plan to ensure that it continues to meet your needs and reflects any changes in your life circumstances.

Estate and succession planning can be complex and overwhelming, but by taking action and working with professionals, you can create a plan that provides for your loved ones and leaves a lasting legacy. Whether you're a middle-class family or a high-net-worth individual, estate planning is an essential part of ensuring your family's financial future and preserving your legacy for generations to come.

In the wake of my family's heartbreaking losses, I embarked on a journey of discovery and education, delving into the intricacies of estate planning and probate law. Through my experiences, I came to understand that estate planning is not just about preserving and protecting wealth; it is about establishing a lasting legacy. It is about passing down not only financial assets but also the values, memories, and work ethic that define us. By crafting a comprehensive estate plan, we can ensure that our loved ones are not burdened with unnecessary disputes and expenses and that our legacy extends far beyond the material realm. I hope that this book has provided you with the knowledge and inspiration to embark on your own wealth journey, one that encompasses not only the preservation of wealth but the preservation of family values, memories, and the enduring spirit that will shape generations to come.

Glossary

1. **Asset:** An asset refers to any item of value that an individual or entity owns or controls, which has the potential to generate economic benefits in the future. Assets can include tangible items such as real estate, vehicles, equipment, and inventory, as well as intangible items such as cash, stocks, bonds, intellectual property, and rights to receive payments. In the context of estate planning and succession planning, assets play a crucial role in determining their distribution, transfer, and management according to the wishes of the owner or as prescribed by applicable laws and legal arrangements.

2. **Beneficiary:** A person or entity named in a will, trust, or insurance policy who is entitled to receive assets or benefits upon the death of the decedent.

3. **Business Succession:** The planning and preparation for the transfer of ownership and management of a business from one owner or generation to the next. It involves determining the future leadership, ownership structure, and continuity of the business.

4. **Buy-Sell Agreement:** A legally binding contract that outlines the terms and conditions for the transfer of ownership interests in a business in the event of specified triggering events, such as the death, disability, retirement, or withdrawal of an owner.

5. **Charitable Remainder Trust (CRT):** A trust that allows individuals to donate assets to a charitable organization while retaining an income stream from those assets during their lifetime. Upon the donor's death, the remaining assets in the trust pass to the designated charity.

6. **Estate Plan:** A comprehensive strategy that includes various legal documents and arrangements to manage a person's assets during their lifetime and control their distribution after death, while minimizing taxes and ensuring the protection of beneficiaries.

7. **Estate Tax:** A tax imposed on the transfer of a deceased person's assets to their beneficiaries. The tax is based on the value of the estate and may vary depending on the jurisdiction.

8. **Executor:** A person named in a will or appointed by the court to carry out the instructions of the deceased person, including managing the estate, paying debts, and distributing assets to beneficiaries.

9. **Family Governance:** The establishment of structures, rules, and processes to facilitate effective communication, decision-making, and continuity within a family, especially in the context of wealth management, estate planning, and succession planning.

10. **Family Limited Partnership (FLP):** A legal entity

that combines elements of a partnership and a corporation, allowing family members to pool assets, protect family wealth, and facilitate efficient transfer of ownership and control across generations.

11. **Guardian:** A person appointed to take care of minor children or incapacitated adults and make decisions about their well-being and financial affairs.

12. **Healthcare Proxy:** A legal document that designates a person to make medical decisions on behalf of another person if they are unable to do so themselves.

13. **Intestate:** The condition of dying without a valid will. In such cases, the distribution of assets is determined by the laws of intestacy in the jurisdiction.

14. **Irrevocable Life Insurance Trust (ILIT):** A trust specifically designed to own a life insurance policy, removing the policy's proceeds from the insured's taxable estate and providing liquidity to cover estate taxes or fund other estate planning objectives.

15. **Letter of Intent:** A document that outlines an individual's wishes, instructions, and preferences regarding the distribution of assets, succession planning, and other matters. Although not legally binding, it provides guidance and clarity to family members and executors.

16. **Living Trust:** A trust created during the lifetime of the grantor, allowing them to retain control over their assets while providing for a smooth transfer of those assets to beneficiaries upon their death, bypassing probate.

17. **Living Will:** A legal document that outlines an individual's preferences regarding medical treatment and end-of-life care if they become unable to communicate or make decisions.

18. **Power of Attorney:** A legal document that grants authority to a person (the agent or attorney-in-fact) to act on behalf of another person (the principal) in managing financial, legal, or health matters.

19. **Probate:** The legal process where a court validates a will, appoints an executor, and oversees the distribution of assets to beneficiaries. It can be time-consuming and costly, but the extent of probate varies depending on state laws and the complexity of the estate.

20. **Succession Planning:** The process of identifying and preparing individuals to take over leadership roles and responsibilities within an organization or family business. It involves ensuring a smooth transition of power and assets from one generation to the next.

21. **Trust:** A legal arrangement where a person (the settlor) transfers their assets to a trustee who manages and

distributes those assets to beneficiaries according to the terms of the trust.

22. **Will:** A legal document that outlines how a person's assets and properties should be distributed after their death. It also allows individuals to name guardians for minor children and specify their funeral and burial wishes.

Please note that legal definitions and terminology may vary based on jurisdiction. Consulting with a qualified estate planning attorney is recommended to fully understand the specific legal implications and interpretations of these terms in your area.

About the Author

Monique D. Hayes is a renowned business attorney. She is a partner in the business law firm, DGIM Law, PLLC. She centers her practice on wealth preservation and protection, including business succession planning. In 2020, she founded Estates Made Easy, an AI-driven digital platform for estate planning. The platform allows for self-driven intergenerational wealth transfer taking into account diverse cultural priorities that impact financial and family planning.

Monique has the rare benefit of experience in both private and public practice. This provides her with a broad understanding of the business and economic landscapes, handling the most complex matters. Her extensive experience includes claim prosecution, asset sales and acquisitions, financial transactions, fraud litigation, restructuring, due diligence, transactional matters, and more.

A balanced approach and innovative mindset greatly support Monique's practice. She regularly provides results-driven counsel to principals, fiduciaries, and both for-profit and non-profit corporations involved in commercial transactions, litigation, and succession planning.

As a leading attorney, board certified in Business Bankruptcy Law recognized as one of the Best Lawyers in America, and ranked by Florida SuperLawyers and Florida

Trend as a "Legal Elite," Monique's impressive professional recognitions are a result of her passion for the law and commitment to excellence. She is a member of the American Bar Association's Business Law Section Council. She is co-chair of the Section's Chapter 11 Sub-Committee. Monique is frequently called upon to provide insight on developments in the law via publications and speaking engagements. She also serves as an adjunct professor at the University of Miami School of Law.

Monique's deep-rooted passion for philanthropy and supporting women and underrepresented groups in the business community, both as a volunteer and leader, is evident in all her commitments. She is a former chair of the International Womens Insolvency and Restructuring Confederation (IWIRC), Florida Network, and past president of the Wilkie D. Ferguson, Jr. Bar Association (a National Bar Association affiliate). She is the Founding Director and Board Chair of Aire Ventures, Inc., a social impact venture studio focused on scaling technology and innovation solutions to systemic gaps in access, opportunity, and racial equity.

Monique is a Past Chair of the University of South Florida (USF) Alumni Association Board of Directors (2021-2022). She regularly contributes her time and talents to other local and national organizations, a rewarding endeavor for which she remains steadfast—as service is part of her DNA.

Early in her career, Monique realized that as a bankruptcy attorney, she would be able to meet her highest objective, "to do well and to do good." Before entering private practice,

Monique served as a law clerk to Hon. Laurel M. Isicoff, Chief Judge of the United States Bankruptcy Court for the Southern District of Florida.

www.moniquedhayes.com

www.ingramcontent.com/pod-product-compliance
Lightning Source LLC
Chambersburg PA
CBHW071606200326
41519CB00021BB/6894